TURNING POINTS

THE ASSASSINATION OF MARTIN LUTHER KING JR.

BY VALERIE BODDEN

CREATIVE EDUCATION • CREATIVE PAPERBACKS

Published by Creative Education and Creative Paperbacks
P.O. Box 227, Mankato, Minnesota 56002
Creative Education and Creative Paperbacks are imprints of
The Creative Company
www.thecreativecompany.us

Design and production by The Design Lab
Art direction by Rita Marshall
Printed in China

Photographs by Corbis (AP, Bettmann, Hulton-Deutsch Collection,
Flip Schulke), Creative Commons Wikimedia (Arnold Newman/U.S.
Federal Government, Birmingham, AL Police Dept., DavGreg, Dumarest,
FBI), Flickr (Joe Brusky), Library of Congress (Russell Lee, Warren K.
Keffler), Shutterstock (catwalker, M DOGAN)

Library of Congress Cataloging-in-Publication Data
Bodden, Valerie.
The assassination of Martin Luther King Jr. / Valerie Bodden.
p. cm. — (Turning points)
Includes bibliographical references and index.
Summary: A historical account of Martin Luther King's assassination, including
the events leading up to it, the people involved, the conditions of racial tension,
and the lingering aftermath.

ISBN 978-1-60818-747-8 (hardcover)
ISBN 978-1-62832-343-6 (pbk)
ISBN 978-1-56660-782-7 (eBook)
King, Martin Luther, Jr., 1929–1968—Assassination—Juvenile literature.

E185.97.K5 B585 2016
323.092 B—dc23   2016000993

CCSS: RI.5.1, 2, 3, 8; RI. 6.1, 2, 4, 7; RH.6-8.3, 4, 5, 6, 7, 8

First Edition HC 9 8 7 6 5 4 3 2 1
First Edition PBK 9 8 7 6 5 4 3 2 1

Cover, main image, and this page: Martin Luther King delivering his
"I Have a Dream" speech in 1963

TABLE *of* CONTENTS

INTRODUCTION

When Martin Luther King Jr. headed to Memphis, Tennessee, in April 1968, he was one of the most beloved—as well as one of the most hated—men in America. Over the past 13 years, his leadership of nonviolent protests had been essential in securing **desegregation** and voting rights for African Americans.

King knew that his position made him a target. He had been jailed 18 times, stabbed, struck in the head by rocks, and attacked by police dogs. Like anyone, King hoped to live a long life. But the 39-year-old expected to die young.

His expectations were fulfilled on April 4. As King stood on the balcony outside his motel room, an assassin fired a single shot into King's neck. Riots broke out across the country and grief-stricken citizens the world over mourned the death of the great **civil rights** leader.

King's 1963 Birmingham mug shot

The American civil rights movement appeared to die with King. Protests petered out, and the country settled into a seeming contentment with the state of race relations. But in 2014, a movement known as Black Lives Matter took up the civil rights call in response to a string of police shootings of unarmed black men. It seemed King's assassination was a turning point with a lasting legacy.

Almost 50 years after giving his "I Have a Dream" speech, King was memorialized in stone on the National Mall.

CHAPTER ONE

THE DREAMER

Rosa Parks's 1955 mug shot

Martin Luther King Jr. didn't plan to spend his life as a civil rights activist. In 1954, he took a position as pastor of the Dexter Avenue Baptist Church in Montgomery, Alabama. The next year, the civil rights movement fell squarely into his city when a 42-year-old African American woman named Rosa Parks was arrested for refusing to give up her bus seat for a white man.

Like most Southern cities, Montgomery required blacks to sit in the back of the bus, while whites sat in the front. And buses weren't the only places blacks and whites were treated differently. Blacks were refused service at white lunch counters, had to go to the back of stores to try on shoes, and even had to drink from separate "colored" water fountains. Although the U.S. Supreme Court had ordered schools to **integrate** in 1954, few had yet done so.

Having grown up in Atlanta, Georgia, King was all too familiar with racism. When he was only six years old, a white friend had been forbidden to play with him because of his skin color. But so far, King had done little to actively fight such discrimination.

Racial segregation was the law of the land from the 1870s until Congress enacted civil rights protections in the 1960s.

Now, however, black leaders across the city formed the Montgomery Improvement Association (MIA) to organize a bus **boycott**. They asked King to head the organization. At the MIA's first public meeting on December 5, 1955, King stood in front of a crowd of 4,000 people and announced: "We are here … because first and foremost we are American citizens, and we are determined to apply our citizenship to the fullness of its meaning." King assumed the bus boycott would last only a few weeks. But it went on for nearly a year before the Supreme Court declared bus **segregation** illegal.

King's first civil rights victory swept him into the national spotlight. He was featured in magazines and appeared on television shows. African Americans around the country began to pin their hopes for a civil rights revolution on him. King was sometimes overwhelmed by the responsibility. But he realized he had an important role to play. "History has thrust something upon me from which I cannot turn away," he told his congregation.

Building on the success in Montgomery, King helped to found the Southern Christian Leadership Conference (SCLC). He and his wife Coretta moved to Atlanta, where SCLC headquarters were set up. There, King also served with his father as co-pastor of Ebenezer Baptist Church. He traveled the country on

Even after segregationists bombed King's Montgomery home, participants in the bus boycott remained peaceful.

behalf of the SCLC to deliver speeches on race relations and took part in demonstrations for civil rights in cities across the South.

In all of his activities, King followed a strict policy of nonviolence. He believed that nonviolent measures such as **sit-ins**, marches, and acts of **civil disobedience** were the best weapons in the fight against racism. "Nonviolence is a powerful and just weapon," he said. "It is a weapon unique in history, which cuts without wounding and ennobles the man who wields it. It is a sword that heals."

Over the years, King had many notable successes. In the spring of 1963, he led a seven-week campaign to desegregate stores and public facilities in Birmingham, Alabama. Soon afterward, he delivered his now-famous "I Have a Dream" speech in Washington, D.C. Standing before a crowd of 200,000 people, King declared, "I have a dream that my four little children will one day live in a nation where they will not be judged by the color of their skin but by the content of their character." In 1965, King led a march in Selma, Alabama, to help register black voters. Although the 14th and 15th Amendments had given blacks equal status as citizens and the right to vote, in many Southern cities, whites used threats, violence, **poll taxes**, and reading tests to keep blacks from exercising that right.

In both Birmingham and Selma, King and other demonstrators were jailed and beaten back by police officers. Such acts were recorded by TV crews and viewed in homes across the country on the evening news. People everywhere became outraged. President Lyndon B. Johnson used that disapproval—as well as the nation's desire to honor assassinated president John F. Kennedy—to convince Congress to pass the **Civil Rights Act of 1964** and the **Voting Rights Act of 1965**.

King's successes boosted his popularity around the world. In 1963, *Time* magazine named King Man of the Year. The next year, King was awarded the Nobel Peace Prize.

An engraving on the steps of the Lincoln Memorial marks the place where King stood as he delivered his famed speech.

But not everyone loved King. In cities where his efforts failed to produce results, many blacks felt disappointed and betrayed. Many young African Americans disagreed with King's nonviolent methods. They formed their own movements calling for black power. "I believe it's a crime for anyone who is being brutalized to continue to accept that brutality without doing something to defend himself," said Malcolm X, leader of a movement for **black nationalism**.

By 1967, King had also begun to lose the backing of some of his longtime allies, including

POINTING OUT

LETTER FROM A BIRMINGHAM JAIL

*While jailed during the Birmingham campaign, King received a letter from several local white clergymen. It urged blacks to wait patiently for equality. King responded with a 20-page letter that would later be recognized as one of his greatest writings. In it, he wrote, "For years now I have heard the word 'Wait!'... This 'Wait' has almost always meant 'Never.'... We have waited for more than 340 years for our **constitutional** and God-given rights.... I guess it is easy for those who have never felt the stinging darts of segregation to say, 'Wait.'... When you are forever fighting a degenerating sense of 'nobodiness'—then you will understand why we find it difficult to wait."*

President Johnson. Many were angered when King spoke out against U.S. involvement in Vietnam. Nearly every major American newspaper rejected King's antiwar stance. The *Washington Post* went so far as to write, "Many who have listened to him with respect will never again accord him the same confidence." Most said he should stick to civil rights.

Despite such criticism, King was determined to attack another problem area: poverty. At the November 1967 meeting of the SCLC, he announced his vision for the Poor People's Campaign, which would bring poor people of all races to camp on the National Mall the next spring. They would demand that the government spend $30 billion a year to stamp out poverty and provide affordable housing. Although his staff was skeptical about the campaign, King saw the effort as the most significant of his career. "I'm not only concerned about the black poor," he said. "I'm concerned about the white poor. I'm concerned about the Puerto Rican poor, the Indian poor. I'm concerned about the Mexican-American poor. We are going to grapple with the problem of poor people … black and white together."

But in March 1968, with planning for the Poor People's Campaign underway, King received a call from an old friend named James Lawson. Lawson was leading a **strike** of African American garbage workers in Memphis, and he wanted to know if King could stop by to offer his support. King's staff members argued that going to Memphis would distract from preparations for the Poor People's Campaign. But King thought the garbage workers were the very kind of people the campaign was meant to help.

He would go to Memphis.

With one in seven citizens living in poverty in the 1960s, the Poor People's Campaign sought to spur government action by holding marches and encampments.

CHAPTER TWO

THE PROMISED LAND

By the time King reached Memphis on March 18, 1968, the strike there had been going on for five weeks. It had all started when two garbage workers were crushed to death in the back of their garbage truck. A few days later, the city's 1,100 sanitation workers—along with about 200 sewer and drainage employees—decided to strike. They were fed up with unsafe working conditions and minuscule wages. Most made only 80 cents an hour and couldn't even afford to feed their families. In addition, the workers—who were all African American—were expected to call their white managers "sir." The managers, however, often addressed the workers with the disrespectful term "boy." According to sanitation worker Clinton Burrows, it was "like they were working on a plantation, doing what the master said." The strikers carried signs that read, "I AM A MAN."

King's arrival in Memphis thrilled the crowd of more than 15,000 who had gathered at Mason Temple to hear him speak. He told the people, "What does it profit a man to be able to eat at an integrated lunch counter if he doesn't have enough money to buy a hamburger?… If we are going to get equality, if we are going to get adequate wages, we are going to have to struggle for it." Then,

The strikers' I AM A MAN signs took inspiration from the motto of the 1700s British anti-slavery movement: "Am I not a man and a brother?"

Though the march began peacefully, violence quickly erupted; dozens were injured in the chaos that ensued.

energized by the crowd's enthusiastic response, King said he would come back later in the month to lead a march through the city's streets.

True to his word, King returned to Memphis on March 28. But as soon as he arrived on that stifling day, he knew that something was "just wrong." Rather than standing peacefully, the crowd of 15,000 jostled and pushed one another. The march started anyway, but it hadn't gotten far before cries of "black power" rang out from the back of the crowd, along with the sound of shattering glass. Police acted quickly to blockade the remainder of the march's route, and organizers tried to turn the crowd back.

Meanwhile, a police officer escorted King to a hotel, where he watched live television coverage of the march in horror. Young people broke store windows, hurled bottles and bricks, and looted stores. The police chased them down, beating and spraying Mace at both the perpetrators and innocent marchers trying to flee the chaos. A despairing King wondered if he had lost the battle after all. "We live in a sick nation," he told his friend and colleague Ralph Abernathy. "Maybe we just have to give up and let violence take its course. Maybe people will listen to the voice of violence. They certainly won't listen to us."

Ralph Abernathy

King went back to Atlanta in a deep depression. But he soon revived and began to plan another trip to Memphis. He knew that unless he could lead a peaceful rally there, the Poor People's Campaign in Washington, D.C., was doomed.

King returned to Memphis on April 3. That night, he spoke to a crowd of 3,000 at Mason Temple. In the midst of a raging storm, with thunder shaking the building and tornado sirens wailing, King delivered one of the most powerful speeches of his life, now known as "I've Been to the Mountaintop." He mentioned that he had received plenty of death threats upon his arrival in Memphis, but he couldn't worry about those. "Well, I don't know what will happen now," he said. "We've got some difficult days ahead. But it really doesn't matter with me now, because I've been to the mountaintop.... Like anybody, I would like to live a long life.... But I'm not concerned about that now.... [God's] allowed me to go up to the mountain. And I've looked over and I've *seeeeen* the Promised Land! I may not get there with you. But I want you to know tonight, that we, as a people, *will* get to the Promised Land!" When he finished, King had tears in his eyes, as did many in the crowd. Others jumped to their feet, cheering and clapping. "It seemed like he reached down and pulled everything out of his heart," one sanitation worker said.

King spent most of the next day meeting with his staff in his room at the Lorraine Motel. Late in the afternoon, he began to get ready for a dinner hosted by his friend, Reverend Samuel Kyles. Around 5:55 P.M., he stepped onto

The Lorraine Motel in Memphis

Exhausted from his recent travels, King almost did not give his final speech at the Mason Temple.

the open balcony outside his second-floor room and stood talking to friends who had gathered in the parking lot below. About six minutes later, as King was turning to step back toward his room, a single loud *pop* rang out.

Some in the parking lot instinctively ducked, fearing the sound might be a gunshot. Others thought it was a car backfiring. Abernathy, who was still inside the room he shared with King, thought it sounded like a firecracker. "All I could see from inside the room were his feet lying out on the balcony, sticking out just beyond the edge of the glass door, you know, and I thought, *Somebody's shootin' up the place*, I thought. *He's lying down like they teach you to do in the service*—but then I heard groans from the people standin' outside in the courtyard, heard hollerin', 'Oh, Lord! Oh, Lord!' And I knew." Abernathy and the others rushed to King, who lay sprawled on the balcony floor, a pool of blood spreading around his head. A single bullet had blown away part of his neck and jaw.

Within moments, police officers who had been enjoying a break at the fire station across the street swarmed the motel, asking where the shots had come from. Nearly everyone pointed toward a brick rooming house to the northwest. An officer ran toward South Main Street. He arrived moments after a man had dropped a mysterious bundle in front of a store. The store owner gave a description of the man and his getaway car.

King's colleagues, including Jesse Jackson (left) and Ralph Abernathy (right), continued to peacefully advocate for civil rights after his death.

By 6:10 P.M., the police dispatcher was broadcasting a description: "Suspect described as young white male, well dressed, believed in late-model white Mustang, going north on Main from scene of shooting." Police cruisers across the city pulled over every white Mustang they encountered. But they didn't find their suspect. Other officers investigated the rooming house, where they collected evidence from the room of a man other residents said had just left, carrying something with him.

POINTING OUT

WILD TIPS

Soon after King's death, Memphis's newspapers and city council offered a $100,000 reward for information leading to the arrest of his murderer. The FBI was swamped with tips from people claiming to have seen the killer (whose photo was released to the public April 19). Callers from South Carolina, California, Missouri, Colorado, and elsewhere said they had seen him. One woman said the suspect "looked an awful lot like my ex-husband." Another thought it could be her son. Others claimed to have information that the killer was spirited out of the country by the Central Intelligence Agency (CIA) or was being hidden by the **Ku Klux Klan** *(KKK).*

One year after King's death, the Lorraine Motel balcony became a memorial site for those who continued to mourn.

ING, JR.
. 4, 1968
NT
HIP CONFERENCE
OTHER.
DREAMER...
...
OME OF HIS DREAMS
NT

Meanwhile, King was rushed to St. Joseph's Hospital, where he arrived at 6:15 P.M. A team of nearly a dozen doctors worked on him for almost an hour. But the bullet had done too much damage. At 7:05 P.M, King was pronounced dead.

POINTING OUT

PROFILE OF AN ASSASSIN

James Earl Ray was born on March 10, 1928, in Alton, Illinois, to a family living in deep poverty. After dropping out of high school, he enlisted in the army. Soon afterward, he was discharged for "ineptness." By the time he was 24, he had turned to a life of crime and was constantly in and out of jail. In April 1967, he escaped from the Missouri State Penitentiary. He spent some time in Los Angeles, where he took dance lessons and graduated from a bartending course, before moving to King's home state of Georgia two weeks before the assassination.

The home of James Earl Ray's father.

CHAPTER THREE

FREE AT LAST

O nly 15 minutes later, President Johnson
received an urgent message informing him of
King's death. The president was stunned—
and worried. "A jumble of anxious thoughts ran through
my mind," he later said. "What does it mean? Was it
the act of one man or a group? Was the assassin black
or white? Would the shooting bring violence, more
catastrophe, and more extremism?" At 9:00 P.M. Eastern
time, Johnson gave a live televised statement to try to
prevent such a response. "I ask every citizen to reject the blind
violence that has struck Dr. King.… We can achieve nothing by lawlessness and
divisiveness among the American people. It is only by joining together…that we
can continue to move toward equality and fulfillment for all of our people."

Lyndon B. Johnson

Despite the president's plea, riots soon broke out in the capital and in more
than 100 cities across the nation, including Chicago, Baltimore, and Detroit.
Young leaders of the black power movement declared the time of nonviolence
over. "King was the last prince of nonviolence [and] nonviolence is now a dead
philosophy," said Floyd McKissick of the Congress of Racial Equality (CORE).

Rioters' violent reactions to King's death resulted in millions of dollars' worth in damages.

Across the country, mayors imposed dusk-to-dawn curfews and banned alcohol and firearms sales to curb riotous behavior.

"The next Negro to advocate nonviolence should be torn to bits by the black people!"

Although King's colleagues continued to urge calm, they couldn't hold back the tide of anger. "King's assassination is like striking a match and it hits the gasoline," author Gerald Posner said of the event in a 2010 interview. "In major black neighborhoods across the country, there are riots, dozens dead, thousands wounded, thousands arrested." In many cities, the violence continued for 10 days and was put down only with the help of the National Guard and regular Army troops.

According to sociologist and author Michael Eric Dyson, the raw grief experienced by blacks in the wake of King's murder was because "it felt like *our* murder. King's death felt like the death of black progress, the death of black justice, the death of black hope, because its most passionate voice had been sniped into silence." Even as fires continued to burn in American cities, people around the world expressed their sadness as well. "It is with profound grief that we have learned the shocking news of the death of Dr. Martin Luther King, whose valiant struggles for the cause of human dignity shall long be remembered by all peace-loving peoples," wrote Haile Selassie, emperor of Ethiopia. Newspapers in Kenya said the assassination "once again reminds the world of the sick society America is." Closer to home, King's SCLC colleague, Reverend Jesse Jackson, remarked that King had "been a buffer

… between the black community and white community. The white people do not know it, but the white people's best friend is dead."

Not everyone agreed, however. South Carolina senator Strom Thurmond, one of King's most vocal opponents, told a reporter, "I hesitate to say anything bad about the dead, but I do not share a high regard for Dr. King. He only *pretended* to be nonviolent." West Virginia senator Robert Byrd agreed and even hinted that King deserved his fate. "One cannot preach nonviolence, and, at the same time, advocate defiance of the law…. For to defy the law is to invite violence."

Despite such sentiments, Sunday, April 7, was declared a national day of mourning. Flags outside all federal buildings were ordered to fly at half-staff. It was the first time in U.S. history that a private citizen had been honored in this way. The Academy Awards were postponed until after King's funeral. So were the National Hockey League (NHL) playoff games and the season openers of several Major League Baseball (MLB) teams.

On Monday, April 8, an estimated 20,000 people lined up to complete King's planned march in Memphis. Among them were King's wife and his oldest children. In honor of King, marchers proceeded in complete silence. After the march, Coretta Scott King spoke to the crowd. "How many men must die before we can really have a free and true and peaceful society?" she asked.

Coretta Scott King and her children, along with prominent civil rights leaders, led the strikers on a peaceful march through Memphis.

"How long will it take? If we can catch the spirit and the true meaning of this experience, I believe that this nation can be transformed into a society of love, of justice, peace, and brotherhood where all men can really be brothers."

The next day, 150,000 people gathered in Atlanta to say a final goodbye to the slain civil rights leader. Among them were Memphis sanitation workers, along with world leaders, government officials, and celebrities. Another 120 million people watched the funeral on television. Schools and government offices across the country shut down. Even the New York Stock Exchange suspended trading for the day.

The funeral began with a service at Ebenezer Baptist Church. One of the last sermons King ever delivered there served as his eulogy. In it, he said he wanted to be remembered as someone who "tried to love and serve humanity." Afterward, King's coffin was pulled by mule-drawn wagon—a symbol of the poor people he worked so hard to help—to Morehouse College. There, King's longtime mentor and retired Morehouse president, Dr. Benjamin E. Mays, spoke of King's legacy. "I make bold to assert that it took more courage for Martin Luther to practice nonviolence than it took his assassin to fire the fatal shot," Mays said. "He belonged to the world and to mankind. Now he belongs to posterity." Following the service, King was buried at South View

As they followed the mule-drawn wagon to Morehouse College, mourners sang spirituals such as "We Shall Overcome."

Cemetery, until his body could be relocated near his church. His crypt was inscribed "Free at last, Free at last, Thank God Almighty I'm Free at last."

Meanwhile, as the country said goodbye to King, the Federal Bureau of Investigation (FBI) continued its hunt for his killer. The bundle that had been dropped in front of a store contained a rifle, binoculars, a pocket-sized transistor radio, clothing, and other items. Over the next 2 months, more than 3,500 FBI agents stationed in field offices across the country took part in what would become the agency's largest-ever manhunt.

POINTING OUT

PROTECTING A KILLER

Once James Earl Ray was in custody, the U.S. government took extraordinary measures to protect him. They didn't want another Lee Harvey Oswald on their hands. (Oswald had been murdered only two days after being arrested for the assassination of president John F. Kennedy.) Ray's arrival in the U.S. was carried out at night, in secret. He was driven to Memphis's Criminal Courts building in an armored car. In his prison cell, the lights were kept on 24 hours a day, and microphones and cameras constantly monitored him. He was delivered a random plate of food from the prison kitchen, so no one could poison him.

WANTE

CIVIL RIGHTS - CONSPIR
INTERSTATE FLIGHT - ROB
JAMES EARL R

After escaping from the Missouri State Penitentiary in 1967, Ray used the alias Eric Starvo Galt as he traveled around North America.

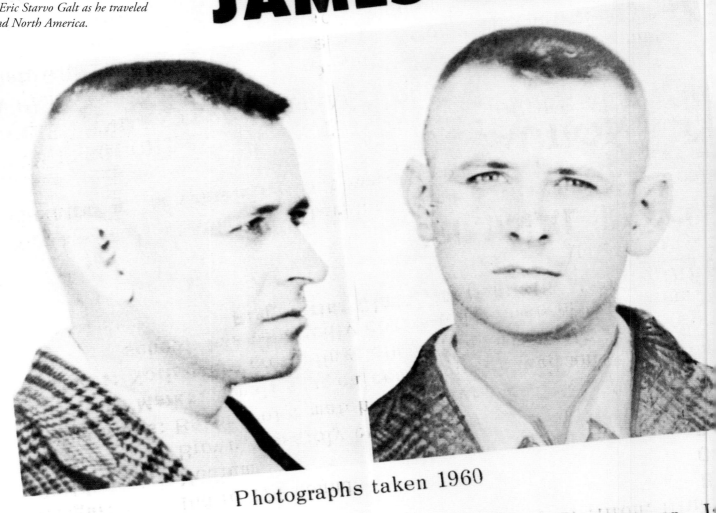

Photographs taken 1960

Aliases: Eric Starvo Galt, W. C. Herron, Harvey Lowmyer, J
Walton, James Walyon, John Willard, "Jim,"

DESCRIPTION

born March 10, 1928, at Quincy or Alton, Illin

FBI No. 405,942 G

Photograph taken 1968
(eyes drawn by artist)
McBride, James O'Conner, James

not supported by birth records)
Blue
Medium

THE DANGER OF A SNEEZE

In 1958, a black woman stabbed King with a seven-inch (17.8 cm) letter opener. Doctors painstakingly removed the sharp instrument. Afterward, they said that if King had so much as sneezed before the surgery, the letter opener would have killed him. As he was recovering, King received a letter from a white student saying, "I'm so happy that you didn't sneeze." In his April 3, 1968, speech in Memphis, King referenced that event, saying, "I am so happy that I didn't sneeze." If he had, he would have missed out on the many great moments in the fight for civil rights.

The evidence helped officers figure out the killer's movements during the days before the shooting. They tracked down the store in Birmingham, Alabama, where he purchased the gun. They found his white Mustang abandoned near a housing project in Atlanta. Eventually, fingerprints led them to their man: James Earl Ray, a 40-year-old white male who had escaped from prison the previous year.

By May, the FBI had traced Ray's movements to Canada. Canadian authorities were able to determine that Ray had traveled to London on a falsified passport. Finally, on June 8, authorities at London's Heathrow Airport apprehended James. It had taken 65 days to catch King's killer.

CHAPTER FOUR

CARRYING ON THE CAUSE

Although many people applauded the work of the FBI in capturing Ray, others doubted they had gotten the right man. Ray was a career thief who had never before shown the desire or the ability to commit murder. At the very least, many said, Ray must have been part of a larger **conspiracy**. Some said Ray was paid off by the KKK or other white supremacist groups. Others suggested that black militants had killed King so that they could take over the civil rights movement. Still others blamed the U.S. government, pointing to FBI director J. Edgar Hoover's well-known dislike of King, which had led him to illegally monitor the civil rights activist for years.

Conspiracy rumors flared up again in March 1969, when Ray pleaded guilty to King's murder. To many, it seemed like a cover-up. "Nothing but outrage and suspicion can follow the handling of this long-delayed and instantly snuffed-out trail," the *New York Times* printed in an editorial. "The question still cries for an answer: Was there a conspiracy to kill Dr. King and who was in it?"

Participants in the Poor People's Campaign encamped on the National Mall read about Ray's apprehension in the papers.

Ray added to that suspicion when, three days later, he **recanted**, saying his lawyer had pressured him to enter the guilty plea. He now claimed he had been part of a plot orchestrated by a mysterious man named Raoul. Many—including King's family—came to believe him. After Ray died in prison in 1998, Coretta Scott King issued a statement. "America will never have the benefit of Mr. Ray's trial, which would have produced new revelations about the assassination … as well as establish the facts concerning Mr. Ray's innocence." The King family held that the U.S. government was responsible for King's murder.

POINTING OUT

FIGHTING FOR A HOLIDAY

Nearly every year from 1968 to 1983, a bill to establish a holiday honoring Martin Luther King Jr. was introduced to Congress. But every year it failed to pass. Few of those who opposed the holiday opposed King himself. Instead, many worried about the expense of another federal holiday. It would cost an estimated $195 million to give federal employees a paid day off. Others worried that it was unfair to honor King when other black leaders might deserve a holiday as well. Despite such objections, in 1983, Congress officially declared the third Monday in January Martin Luther King Jr. Day.

Ray asserted his innocence until his death, but because he had officially pled guilty, he could not appeal his case.

After King's death, President Johnson was finally able to rouse Congress into passing the Civil Rights Act of 1968—a bill two years in the making.

Over the years, scores of lawyers, journalists, and members of the House Select Committee on Assassinations (HSCA) have reexamined the evidence. Most have come to the conclusion that Ray alone killed King. Even so, in 2008, a reported 88 percent of black Americans and 50 percent of whites still believed King's death was part of a larger secret plan.

One reason conspiracy theories remain so popular is that no motive was ever given for Ray's execution of King. Some contend he did it for money. Several racist groups and individuals had placed bounties on King's head, and Ray may have thought he could cash in on one. Or, Ray may have just wanted the notoriety. "I think that Ray felt, 'Now I'm a big man. I'm no longer a loser.... I made the FBI's top ten [most wanted list].... I slew the dreamer,'" said national news anchor Dan Rather. According to journalist Marshall Frady, "Much of the urge to believe that King had to have been slain by a conspiracy arises ... from a reluctance to accept ... that so much could have been effaced [wiped out] through so paltry an agent."

Whatever the reason for King's death, many were determined to ensure that it was not in vain. Only a week after the assassination, President Johnson signed the Civil Rights Act of 1968, also known as the Fair Housing Act. The law made it illegal to discriminate on the basis of

After her husband's death, Coretta Scott King became more involved in the civil rights movement and encouraged all women to do the same.

race in home sales and rental agreements. Republican senator Jacob Javits of New York called the bill a "living memorial" to King.

In May 1968, King's followers offered another living tribute as they carried out his wishes for the Poor People's Campaign. More than 2,000 poor people from across the country thronged to the nation's capital to live in makeshift plywood and canvas shelters. They demanded a minimum yearly income, an end to hunger, and a plan to rebuild poor inner city areas. The campaign got off to a strong start with marches and sit-ins. But by the second week, it had devolved into violence. After six weeks, the demonstrators were forced to leave. None of their demands had been met.

A 1999 postage stamp

The failure of the Poor People's Campaign seemed to prove just how essential King had been in the civil rights movement. Although leaders such as Jesse Jackson continued the fight for equality, King's death seemed to mark an end to large-scale racial protests.

But the movement had many lasting effects. Within 15 years of King's death, there was no public sign of segregation in the South. Blacks were elected to political offices in places where they had once been kept from voting. In 2008, King's vision of equality seemed to be realized when Barack Obama became the first black president in U.S. history.

King's influence has been felt elsewhere in the world as well. In 1987, students in South Korea took to the streets to demand their **dictator** set up fair elections. In 1989, the **communist** Soviet Union fell apart as strikers sang "We Shall Overcome," a song that had been popular at King's marches. That same year, Chinese students held their own sit-in in Tiananmen Square to protest their country's lack of basic freedoms.

Today, streets, schools, and parks around the world are named after King. He is the only non-president honored with a memorial on the National Mall and the only non-president recognized with a national holiday. Visitors to Memphis can tour the Lorraine Motel, which has been converted into the National Civil Rights Museum. Across the street, tourists can view the room from which Ray fired the lethal shot. Farther south, in Atlanta, Coretta Scott King established the Martin Luther King Jr. Center for Nonviolent Social Change. The King Center, which is today headed by King's youngest daughter, Bernice King, studies and promotes nonviolent social action.

In August 2014, the King Center urged the country to remain calm in the wake of the police shooting of Michael Brown, a young, unarmed black man, in Ferguson, Missouri. But rioting broke out in Ferguson and elsewhere. Police responded with tear gas and military gear. Over the following months, nationwide attention was drawn to several cases of police shootings of unarmed black men.

Soon, a new movement, known as Black Lives Matter, was born. Protesters used many of the same tactics King had used—including sit-ins and civil disobedience. "The movement is rooted in

The "Black Lives Matter" mantra was invoked at many gatherings in 2015, including a candlelight vigil in Madison, Wisconsin.

protests," said activist DeRay Mckesson, echoing King's philosophy. "When the protests stop, we lose the power. The structure has no place for us, which is why we protest. When protests end, the movement ends."

Some thought the movement died nearly 50 years ago with its most famous fighter. But as King once said, "If I am stopped, this movement will not be stopped." Today, more than ever, the truth of these words can be felt as the revived civil rights movement rekindles this turning point in American history.

January 15, 1929	Martin Luther King Jr. is born in Atlanta.
September 20, 1944	At the age of 15, King enters Morehouse College in Atlanta.
June 18, 1953	King marries Coretta Scott; the couple eventually has four children.
December 1, 1955	Rosa Parks is arrested for failing to give up her bus seat to a white man. King leads a bus boycott in response.
April 16, 1963	King writes his now-famous "Letter from a Birmingham Jail."
August 28, 1963	King delivers his "I Have a Dream" speech to a crowd of 200,000 in Washington, D.C.
December 10, 1964	King, an "undaunted champion of peace," is awarded the Nobel Peace Prize for his nonviolent campaign.
March 7, 1965	King joins protests in Selma, Alabama.
December 4, 1967	King and the SCLC publicly announce plans for a Poor People's Campaign in Washington, D.C.
April 4, 1968	King is shot and killed while standing on the balcony of the Lorraine Motel in Memphis.
April 9, 1968	A day after demonstrators carry out a silent march in Memphis in his honor, King is buried in Atlanta.
June 8, 1968	James Earl Ray is apprehended in London and arrested for King's murder.
March 10, 1969	Ray pleads guilty to King's murder but recants three days later.
1979	The House Select Committee on Assassinations confirms James Earl Ray was King's killer.
2014	The Black Lives Matter movement increases its responses to police shootings of unarmed black men.

black nationalism—a militant African American movement that advocates separating from whites and forming black communities that govern themselves

boycott—to refuse to use or buy a product or service as an act of protest or to show support for a cause

civil disobedience—nonviolent refusal to obey a law as an act of protest because the law is considered unfair

civil rights—rights of all people; the civil rights movement was a political movement of the 1950s and 1960s with the goal of attaining equal treatment for racial minorities

Civil Rights Act of 1964—a bill signed into law on July 2, 1964, outlawing discrimination based on race, religion, or national origin

communist—involving a system of government in which all property and business is owned and controlled by the state, with the goal of creating a classless society

conspiracy—a secret plan carried out by two or more people

constitutional—having to do with the system of laws and principles that defines how a specific government or institution functions

desegregation—the process of ending segregation, or the separation of people by race

dictator—a ruler with complete power, who often rules by force

integrate—to end segregation by intermixing majority and minority populations; school integration involved allowing African American students to attend schools with white students

Ku Klux Klan—a secret society that believed whites were superior to all other races and committed acts of terrorism against blacks

poll taxes—money a person has to pay in order to vote

recanted—publicly took back something that was said earlier

segregation—the process of separating people by race; in the U.S., segregation meant that African Americans had to ride at the back of buses, eat in separate dining establishments, and attend separate schools

sit-ins—protests in which demonstrators sit in a public place such as a government building or store and refuse to leave

strike—the refusal of a group of employees to work until an employer meets demands such as higher pay or better working conditions

Voting Rights Act of 1965—a bill signed into law on August 6, 1965, designed to prohibit racial discrimination in voting; the act outlawed the use of tests to determine voter eligibility

Chappell, David L. *Waking from the Dream: The Struggle for Civil Rights in the Shadow of Martin Luther King, Jr.* New York: Random House, 2014.

Dyson, Michael Eric. *April 4, 1968: Martin Luther King, Jr.'s Death and How It Changed America.* New York: Perseus, 2008.

Frady, Marshall. *Martin Luther King Jr.: A Life.* New York: Penguin, 2002.

King, Coretta Scott. *My Life with Martin Luther King, Jr.* New York: Holt, Rinehart, and Winston, 1969.

King, Martin Luther, Jr. *Why We Can't Wait.* 1963. Boston: Beacon, 2010.

Posner, Gerald. *Killing the Dream: James Earl Ray and the Assassination of Martin Luther King, Jr.* New York: Random House, 1998.

Sides, Hampton. *Hellhound on His Trail: The Electrifying Account of the Largest Manhunt in American History.* New York: Random House, 2010.

Somashekhar, Sandhya, Wesley Lowery, and Keith L. Alexander. "Black and Unarmed." *Washington Post*, August 8, 2015. http://www.washingtonpost.com/sf/national/2015/08/08/black-and-unarmed/.

History.com: Civil Rights Movement
http://www.history.com/topics/black-history/civil-rights-movement
Watch historical video footage from the civil rights movement.

National Civil Rights Museum: Standing Up
http://civilrightsmuseum.org/standingup/
See what it was like to be a civil rights activist in the 1950s and '60s.

Note: Every effort has been made to ensure that the websites listed above are suitable for children, that they have educational value, and that they contain no inappropriate material. However, because of the nature of the Internet, it is impossible to guarantee that these sites will remain active indefinitely or that their contents will not be altered.

INDEX